Little Books of Guidance
Finding answers to life's big questions!

Also in the series:
What Is Christianity? by Rowan Williams
Who Was Jesus? by James D. G. Dunn
Why Go to Church? by C. K. Robertson
How Can Anyone Read the Bible? by L. William
    Countryman
What About Sex? by Tobias Stanislas Haller, BSG

WHAT HAPPENS WHEN WE DIE?

A Little Book of Guidance

THOMAS G. LONG

Church Publishing
NEW YORK

Unless otherwise noted, the Scripture quotations contained herein are from the New
Revised Standard Version Bible, copyright © 1989 by the Division of Christian
Education of the National Council of Churches of Christ in the U.S.A.
Used by permission. All rights reserved.

Church Publishing
19 East 34th Street
New York, NY 10016
www.churchpublishing.org

Cover design by Jennifer Kopec, 2Pug Design
Typeset by Progressive Publishing Services

Library of Congress Cataloging-in-Publication Data

A record of this book is available from the Library of Congress.

ISBN-13: 978-0-89869-233-4 (pbk.)
ISBN-13: 978-0-89869-264-8 (ebook)

Printed in the United States of America

Contents

Introduction

What happens when we die?

Everyone asks this question sooner or later, sometimes in secret, sometimes in whispers to a friend or loved one, sometimes in bold urgency. What happens when we die? Which is really our way of asking the most personal of all questions: What happens when *I* die?

There are two ways to understand that question. It can mean, "What happens to us *as* we are dying?" What happens to our bodies, our self, our relationships as life is slipping away? It can also mean, "What happens to us *after* we die?" Is there a future for us after this life? Is there life after death? In this small book, we will seek to view the question both ways. Neither way of asking the question evokes easy answers. And we will look in many directions for wisdom. We will seek insight primarily from the Christian faith, but we will also look to contemporary science, to medicine, to philosophy, and to other religious traditions for the knowledge they offer.

1

In the Hour of Our Death

The Fear of Our Mortality

A good friend of mine read the *New York Times* bestselling book *Being Mortal*[1] by Atul Gawande, a surgeon and a professor at Harvard Medical School. The book is a very frank physician's description of what it is like for us, as human beings, to come to the end of life. Dr. Gawande describes what it means to grow old, what it means for our bodies to wear down and to fail, and especially what it means to encounter the inevitable truth that we will all die. When my friend got about halfway through the book, he confessed to me, "You know, this book scares the heck out of me!"

I understand. What frightened my friend about this book, and what would frighten most of us, I suppose, is right there in the book's title: *Being Mortal.* We are all mortal. We will all die. We know that, of course, but until death actually draws near,

3

we know it only in the abstract. There is an old Jewish saying, "Everybody knows they're going to die, but nobody believes it."

When he was seventy-one years old, the former U.S. president Thomas Jefferson wrote to another former president, the seventy-eight-year-old John Adams,

> Our machines have been running seventy or eighty years and we must expect . . . here a pivot, there a wheel, now a pinion, next a spring will be giving way. . . . There is a ripeness of time for death . . . when it is reasonable we should drop off and make room for another growth.[2]

Notice how Jefferson, while frankly admitting that he and Adams will die, still distances himself from the raw reality of it by speaking of death as "reasonable" and using metaphors for body parts such as wheels and springs. What can be so frightening about a book like *Being Mortal* is that the author does not gloss over the biological facts, nor does he disguise the bodily deterioration with metaphors. Our blood vessels narrow and become stiff from calcium buildup, Gawande says, causing the heart to pump harder. By age sixty-five, more than half of us have hypertension. At eighty, we have lost between one-quarter and a half of our muscle weight, and after age eighty-five, 40 percent of us have lost all of our teeth. Gawande goes on:

> Although the processes can be slowed—diet and physical exercise can make a difference—they cannot be stopped. Our functional lung capacity decreases. Our bowels slow down. Our glands stop functioning. Even our brains shrink: at the age of thirty, the brain is a three-pound organ that barely fits inside the skull; by our seventies, gray-matter loss leaves almost an inch of spare room. . . . [A]fter a blow to the head, the brain actually rattles around inside. . . . Processing speeds start decreasing well before age forty. . . . By age eighty-five, working memory and judgment are sufficiently impaired that 40 percent of us have textbook dementia.[3]

In sum, Dr. Gawande forces us to face the truth that what happens to the human body over time is not pretty. We are all aging, and along with aging comes physical and mental diminishment. There's no way around it, no way to stop it. Despite all the vitamins and exercise and healthy diets and strong medicines in the world, our minds and our bodies will ultimately decline and fail; we will all eventually come to the end of our days.

Ways We Respond to Our Mortality

There are three main ways that people in our society respond to this reality of aging and the inevitability of death.

Cultural Denial

When we are young, most of us don't think much about the end of life. It seems so far away that it doesn't even feel real. We know that death happens to people, but to *other* people, to *old* people, but it's not a part of our experience or expectation, not our concern. But, of course, our youth eventually fades, and we do grow older. Even so, we may still try to pretend that we are somehow immune to the aging process, exempt from mortality, that it's not happening to us. Many companies have discovered that there is plenty money to be made in helping people fool themselves that they can beat the mortality clock. Beautiful young people on television and in the movies joke about old people, and the message is clear: to be "old" is an embarrassment, an insult, and an outrage. So we make believe that we can somehow avoid it. "Seventy is the new fifty," we say, lying to ourselves. Or as the commercials on TV reassure us, just a touch of color to take out the grey hair, and we're "still in the game," or just a dab of miracle facial cream to smooth out the wrinkles, and we can be as ageless as supermodel Cindy Crawford.

"There are substances on the market now that claim to prolong life—and people are spending billions on them," said a *New York Times* interviewer to Professor Leonard P. Guarente, an expert on aging at M.I.T.

"Well, that's really simple," replied Guarente. "Any product on the market that claims to extend life—don't believe it."[4]

Indeed, at some point, the inevitability of death becomes harder to deny, the illusion of everlasting life more difficult to maintain . . . and then impossible. In one of Wallace Stegner's novels, there is an elderly man who writes in his Christmas letter that when anybody asks him if he feels like an old man, he says, "No, no. I feel like a young man with something the matter with him."[5] As we age and move inexorably toward life's end, we can't shake the feeling that there's something the matter with us, something wrong about our mortal journey. To be old, we fear, is to be nearing the end, the end of our attractiveness, the end of our usefulness, the end of our strength, the end of our health, the end of our life. But all cosmetic attempts to deny this reality are just that—cosmetic.

Medical Postponement

For scientific medicine, the goal—and often an unquestioned goal—is to postpone aging and death and to extend the length of life as far as we can. Historians tell us that the average citizen of the Roman Empire could expect to live a little less than thirty years. But today, medical science— through antibiotics and surgical breakthroughs, improved hygiene and nutrition—has made it possible for the average citizen of developed nations to live almost three times that long. And there is no reason to think, as we move into the future, that modern medicine will not be able to add higher and higher numbers, longer and longer lives. Some researchers are even contemplating uploading our consciousness into the digital cloud so that when our bodies give way, our minds will go on humming in perpetuity.

We should be grateful, of course, for many of these advances in medicine. Children who a century ago would have died from smallpox or would have been paralyzed by polio now do not have to fear these diseases. Men and women who would have had their lives cut short by tuberculosis now may live long and productive lives. And we can pray that someday the ravages of heart disease, cancer, Alzheimer's, and other diseases will also be a thing of the past.

But there are some darker tones to this medical quest to provide longer and longer lives. First, there is the suspicion that many physicians see the death of a patient as a personal defeat, and, as a result, are willing to perform extreme measures, even at the expense of the quality of life, to keep their patients technically alive. The physician Sherwin Nuland, in his groundbreaking book *How We Die,* pictures a team of doctors, nurses, and technicians desperately attempting to resuscitate a heart attack victim with only the minutest chance of surviving. Despite their furious efforts, the patient's eyes widen into blackness, and the emergency room moves from a mood of "heroic rescue to the gloom of failure." The patient, says Nuland, "dies among strangers: well-meaning, empathetic . . . but strangers nonetheless." Nuland adds, "The only certainty, whether spoken or not, is that the doctors, nurses, and technicians are fighting not only death but their own uncertainties as well."[6]

More and more, the wisest physicians are acknowledging that there is an upper limit to the human life span. No matter how many medical advances are made, and even if cures were developed for every single disease, the human body is not designed to keep striving past about 100 years of age. Science can keep pushing the limits, but there is a brick wall of mortality ahead.[7]

Ironically, the quest of medical science simply to add more time—more minutes, hours, and days—to the human life span, can end up causing more harm than good, cutting people off from the people who love them and from the substance of a meaningful life, adding more days but subtracting the goodness of the days we have.

In an Easter sermon, Pope Benedict XVI wondered what it might be like if medicine were to succeed. What if medicine figured out a way for us to live to, say, 200 or 300 years of age?

> Would that be a good thing? Humanity would become extraordinarily old, there would be no more room for youth. Capacity for innovation would die, and endless life would be no paradise, if anything

a condemnation. The true cure for death must be different. It cannot lead simply to an indefinite prolongation of this current life. It would have to transform our lives from within. It would need to create a new life within us, truly fit for eternity. . . .[8]

Numbering Our Days

In the face of the culture's attempts to deny our mortality and medicine's desire simply to extend the human life span, the Hebrew poet who composed Psalm 90 has a more profound response. He wrote, "So teach us to number our days that we may get a heart of wisdom" (Ps. 90:12 RSV). What the psalmist is asking for is not that the number of his days grow bigger and bigger, but instead that the limits on his life teach him how to value his days and to gain wisdom. In other words, the psalmist asks God for the ability to count each day as precious, to cherish the gift of the days that he has been allotted, so that the psalmist can gain wisdom in the living of those days. The goal is not simply the quantity of life, but the quality of life—the depth and breadth and height of life, not just its length. What makes life good is not just longevity, not just living more and more days, but becoming a certain kind of person, a person of character and depth, a person whose heart is wise before God. As the philosopher and essayist Montaigne said, "The advantage of living is not measured by length, but by use; some men have lived long, and lived little; attend to it while you are in it. It lies in your will, not in the number of years, for you to have lived enough."[9]

It is right at this point that faith must raise a provocative challenge, both to the lies of those who would deny death and to the overreaching ambitions of modern medicine. The reality of our mortality cannot be covered up cosmetically, and while people of faith join with all others in giving thanks for the many ways that medicine gives us strength and health and freedom from unrelenting pain, what must be challenged is the false idea that the *only* way to seek a good life is the never-ending quest for more of it, for more and more days, for longer and longer lives. Lying just beneath the surface of this medical quest for unending life is the false promise, the science fiction dream, even the idolatrous claim, that science and medicine will one day give us immortality, that someday medicine will genetically engineer death out of the human equation—the dream that human beings on biological grounds can live forever and that living forever would be a good thing.

Our quest for immortality, for a life that just goes on and on forever, is actually based on fear, a fear of running out of time.

"I don't think people are afraid of death," said a thirty-year-old man dying of leukemia. "What they are afraid of is the incompleteness of their life."[10] When the *New York Times* columnist Anatole Broyard was dying of cancer, he wrote, "I want to be a good story [for my doctor]."[11] Down deep, that is what all of us fear, that we are incomplete, that the story of who we are supposed to be is not good enough and is never finished. Indeed, fear comes from believing that there is not enough to go around, not enough to finish the story. Not enough time, not enough joy, not enough strength, not enough love, not enough nourishment, not enough me, and not enough grace. We are afraid that we are running out of time; and when the end comes, there will only be nothingness—darkness, an empty hall, a bare table, and an unfinished story. And so we turn in desperation to medicine, pleading, "Give me more time. Give me endless days. Don't let me die. Don't let my life be incomplete." "What I am really afraid of," said the dying man, "is the incompleteness of my life."

But medicine cannot give us immortality, and it cannot even give us a sense of the completeness of life. It can only, at best, postpone the inevitable, prolong life a few more days, a few more months, or a few more years. Only God can give us a sense of completeness; and because God is the one who gives us completeness, from the point of view of faith, it is actually good news that we are not immortal. When we acknowledge that we are mortal—temporary, provisional, unfinished, incomplete—when we gain the deep knowledge that we are limited in days and incomplete in ourselves, this can draw us ever closer to the God who is immortal and who brings our life to completion. That is what the psalmist means when he prays, "Teach us to number our days that we gain a wise heart." Teach us to number our days so that we will gain the wisdom of knowing that our hearts are restless until they rest in God.

Often people will say something like, "I know that one day I will die, but I want to die a dignified death." What this means is that people hope that their deaths, and the deaths of those they love, will be peaceful, serene, and without pain. Unfortunately, death is itself an indignity, and it rarely comes without wreaking its undignified destruction and leaving its cruel marks. As one woman said to the attending physician, after watching her mother die of breast cancer, "It was nothing like the peaceful end I expected. I thought it would be spiritual . . . [but] there was too much pain, too much Demerol. . . . [T]here was no dignity in my mother's death!" Thinking about this remark later, the physician frankly admitted to himself, "I have not often seen much dignity in the process by which we die."[12]

To number our days seeking wisdom, however, points in a different direction. We are not guaranteed a dignified death, but what we are offered is a *sacred* death, a holy death. Jesus did not die a dignified death; he was executed as a criminal by the state, nailed cruelly to a wooden cross. There is little dignity to be found in that. But his life was a sacred death because his life was shaped as an offering given to God, and his life was received by God and redeemed. As Sherwin Nuland said, "The greatest dignity to be found in death is the dignity of the life that preceded it."[13]

The last book that the great philosopher Ernest Becker wrote before his own untimely death at age forty-nine, was *The Denial of Death.* He wrote about our futile attempt as human beings to defeat death by setting up ourselves and our achievements as somehow immortal. But such attempts ultimately come crashing down, and what is left to us? In the last sentence of the book, Becker provides his keenest insight: "The most that any one of us can seem to do is to fashion something—an object or ourselves—and drop it into the confusion, make an offering of it, so to speak, to the life force."[14]

For people of faith, what Becker calls "the life force" is, of course, God, the God of all life. It is in "numbering our days," and in knowing that each day is a gift from the living God, a day to be lived in joy and gratitude, lived in self-giving love, and in the end fashioned as an offering to God, that life is made complete and whole. It is also knowing that when we do not live this way, when our joy turns to bitterness and our gratitude into resentment, that we are finally surrounded by the mercy and forgiveness of God, which redeems even our brokenness.

That is why the first word of Easter, the first word from the risen Christ, is "Do not be afraid." The risen Christ is saying to us, "You are so anxious and fearful about how your life will end. But do not be afraid. *This* is how it ends . . . in resurrection. To belong to me is to be given the gift of an ending to life that you could never achieve in your own power, that no earthly physician can provide, no medicine can produce—the gift of being gathered in glory and joy into the eternal life of God. That is how it ends. So, do not be afraid."

The great Irish poet Seamus Heaney died in 2013 at age seventy-four. After collapsing on a Dublin street, he was rushed to a hospital and then taken into the operating suite, where unfortunately he died before surgery could take place. Minutes before he died, Heaney, the poet who loved and mastered language, communicated his very last words on this earth in a text message sent to his wife, Marie. Two words in Latin: "*Noli timere,*" which means, "Do not be afraid." Heaney learned these words from Jesus, learned them from the biblical story of Easter, where the risen Christ said to his followers, "Do not be afraid" (Matt. 28:10). Heaney was raised in the Catholic Church, but he had his quarrels with the church and even with the faith. Nevertheless, there at the end of his life, these old words came back to him. His mortality drew him toward this ancient affirmation, this scriptural promise, toward the assurance that our restless lives find their rest in God and that we are calmed by the certainty of God's grace. So, "*noli timere;* do not be afraid."

The choir in the church where my family worships has a wonderful and unusual custom. Whenever a member of the congregation is admitted to hospice care and is facing the last few days of life, the choir will go to the hospice to sing to them, to sing the great anthems of faith. This singing is a comfort, yes, but it is more than that. It is a confession of faith that we are surrounded in life and in death by the gospel story, that we do not bear the burden of making our own lives complete. We can be content, even comforted, in our mortality, in our incompleteness, because the completion we desire in life has been provided as a gift from God, the God who was there at the beginning and will be there at the end.

Years ago, a friend of mine was in the hospital dying of cancer. Near the end, she called her pastor and said, "I have been reading the Bible, the place in the book of James where it says if you are sick, you should call the elders of the church for prayer and anointing with oil. I'd like you to come to the hospital and do that for me." Her pastor seemed to hesitate, and my friend asked, "What's wrong?"

"I don't know," he said. "It seems a little like magic, anointing you with oil. I practice ministry, not magic."

My friend became angry. "Look," she said to her pastor, "I am dying. I *know* I am dying. I will probably die in the next few days."

"Then why do you want to be anointed with oil?" he asked.

"Because it will remind me of my baptism," she said. "It will let me know that the Christ who was there for me in the beginning will be standing with me at the end. The Christ who is my alpha will also be the Christ who is my omega." And so it was, that a few days before she died, her pastor and some others from the church came to the hospital to anoint her and to remind her of her baptism and to assure her that in life and in death she was complete and made whole in the grace and mercy of God.

When the well-known Jewish author and neurologist Oliver Sacks turned eighty years old, he wrote an essay in the *New York Times* about his life and what he saw ahead of him. At eighty, Sacks was still strong and productive, and he wrote, "I feel I should be trying to complete my life, whatever 'completing a life' means."[15] Sacks had no way of knowing that only two years later, he would have received a diagnosis of terminal cancer and that his body would be weakening and failing by the day. But Sacks had been given, I would say by God's grace, a heart of wisdom; and just a few months before his death, he wrote another essay in the *New York Times.* This time, though, he knew he was dying, knew he was mortal, and he was not talking about completing his life, but about the Sabbath. "I find my thoughts drifting to the Sabbath," he wrote, "the day of rest, the seventh day of the week, and perhaps the seventh day of one's life as well, when one can feel that one's work is done, and one may, in good conscience, rest."[16]

The Sabbath, of course, is God's gift to us—not *our* achievement, but God's gift. Six days shall we labor and do all our work, but the Sabbath, the seventh day, the completion of all things, the end of all things, is pure grace, pure gift.

Whether we are in the springtime of our life or the winter, the first day of our life's week or the sixth day, whether we are young or old, whether we are in full strength or our bodies are failing, whether we are at the beginning or nearing the end, *noli timere*. We do not need to be afraid. Grace is infinite. The Sabbath banquet is set and waiting. We can number our days, confident that when we come to the end, the risen Christ will be there to receive us, to say to us, "You are home now. You have a place at the table. There is plenty to go around."

On the Other Side of Death's Curtain

Possible Answers to the Question "What Happens after Death?"

Since the very beginning of human history, people have wondered and dreamed about what happens to us after death. Because the dead no longer communicate with the living, we are left to guess what happened to them, and what will happen to us. Do the dead continue to exist? If so, what is that existence like?

In all of our human wondering about life after death, human beings have arrived at five basic answers to the question, what happens after death?

1. Nothing. Some believe that human beings share a common fate with all other living things. Like insects and oak trees and like sparrows and sea coral, humans live out their life spans and then simply cease to be. We are part of a biological life cycle. Our bodies decay like the grass of the field. We become dust and are blended into the humus, the soil out of which other living things spring forth and grow.

2. Immortality of the Soul. Others believe that, while our bodies die, there is something about a human being, namely the soul, that is immortal. When we die, the soul, this spark of the divine, is reunited with its source: God. In previous centuries, people imagined the soul to be a physical entity, and some scientists would conduct experiments where they would weigh a person just before and just after death, trying to calculate the weight of a soul. However, most people today who have a view of the immortality of the soul think of the soul not as a body part, with shape and mass, but as a kind of life force or energy.

3. Reincarnation. This is the idea that the soul, or the cumulative force of one's previous lives, continues to live on, but in another body. Often connected to the concept of reincarnation is the belief that the migration of the soul from body to body offers the chance for the soul's purification. For some ancient Greek philosophers (such as Plato), souls were originally with God and were pure, but souls fell from this state of perfection (they "lost their wings") and descended into corrupt fleshly bodies. Reincarnation, therefore, is the gradual escape of the soul from all embodiment and a step-by-step restoration of the soul as pure and finally disembodied. In Hinduism, writes religion scholar Lisa Miller, the cycle of reincarnation "is affected by karma, a system of cause and effect that we are used to thinking about as rewards, or consequences. Good deeds now will have a salutary bearing on a soul's next life."[17]

4. Resurrection of the Soul. This view of life after death acknowledges that human beings die, and that there is nothing immortal about a human being that survives the experience of death. However, in the power of God, the soul is given new life and brought into a heavenly relationship with God and the souls of the saints. Sometimes, the New Testament Book of Hebrews, with its vision of the heavenly city and "spirits of the righteous made perfect," is seen to support this view of the resurrection of the soul:

You have not come to something that can be touched . . . But you have come to Mount Zion and to the city of the living God, the heavenly Jerusalem, and to innumerable angels in festal gathering, and to the assembly of the firstborn who are enrolled in heaven, and to God the judge of all, and to the spirits of the righteous made perfect, and to Jesus, the mediator of a new covenant, and to the sprinkled blood that speaks a better word than the blood of Abel. (Heb. 12:18–24)

5. Resurrection of the Body. In the main, Christian theology does not subscribe to any of the four views above but instead to the promise of the resurrection of the body. In this view, expressed in the ancient Apostles' Creed ("I believe in . . . the resurrection of the body, and the life everlasting"), human beings are created by the living God and have life only as a gift from God. The book of Genesis pictures this act of creation in this way: "Then the Lord God formed man from the dust of the ground, and breathed into his nostrils the breath of life; and the man became a living being" (Gen. 2:7). Therefore, humans are not immortal souls trapped in fleshly bodies. Rather, humans are made from dust and given the life-giving breath of God. Humans don't *have* bodies; we *are embodied.* When we die, everything about us dies, and if there is to be any life after death, it will come only if God raises us from the dead—raises the whole embodied human being.

This central Christian claim of the resurrection of the body taxes the credulity of many people today, including many Christians. Lisa Miller writes,

> Resurrection is, on the face of it, impossible, the stuff of science-fiction horror stories. It means, literally, to rise again, the revivification of dead flesh, yet this Frankenstein scenario is the bedrock of the Christian story, the defining test of faith. Without it, Jesus would have been another Jewish rebel crucified for his insubordination to the Roman regime.[18]

Actually, Miller doesn't have it quite right. The notion of dead bodies getting up from their graves and walking around, zombie-like, is not what Christians affirm about resurrection, but Miller does recognize that the very idea of the resurrection of the body raises serious questions that need responses. In thinking through these questions, Christian rely on more than just speculation. Christians believe that they can point to the one experience of encountering one who was dead and then raised, namely, Jesus himself.

Looking at Death through the Lens of the Resurrection

The story of Easter and the accounts of the risen Christ encountering his followers, therefore, are the best guides we have to understanding what the resurrection of the body means. Let us pose some of those key questions:

What happens to us at the time of death?—About three o'clock in the afternoon of the day he was crucified, Jesus "breathed his last" (Matt. 27:50). Jesus was dead, completely dead. He was not secretly alive, pretending to be dead. He was not hiding behind a bush in heaven, just waiting for Easter morning so that he could appear again. He was dead and buried, dead as a doornail. And so will it be for all human beings. At some point, we will stop breathing, our hearts will cease beating, all brain activity will end, our bodies will become still and cold, and we will be irretrievably dead. No medicine or magic will be able to revive us.

When Jesus was dead, however, his crumpled and brutalized body was not simply discarded as if it no longer had any worth. In fact, a man named Joseph, who was from the town of Arimathea, about twenty miles from Jerusalem, saw to it that Jesus's body was treated properly and with respect. Matthew says that Joseph of Arimathea was wealthy, Mark that he was a respected leader, Luke that he was good and righteous, and John whispers that he was a secret disciple of Jesus. But what he did that will be remembered is that he recognized that the Roman executioners would have tossed Jesus's body into a common ditch or left it on the roadside for animals to devour, and he was convinced that Jesus's body deserved more respect. So, Joseph asked Pontius Pilate, the Roman governor who was in charge of Jesus's execution, if he could have the body of Jesus. An almost surely puzzled Pilate agreed. Why would anyone want the dead body of a criminal? Joseph teamed up with Nicodemus (who was perhaps another secret disciple) to tenderly prepare the body for burial. They wrapped Jesus's body, along with spices, in a linen cloth and placed him in a newly hewn rock tomb (see John 19:38–42).

This tender and reverent treatment of Jesus's dead body was done, says John, "according to the burial custom of the Jews." This Jewish practice was no mere habit; it grew out of a profound theology of creation. Our bodies are fashioned by God as a part of all that God created in the material world, and even when life is gone, the bodies of the dead are to be treated as tokens and signs of that gift. These are, after all, the bodies that allowed the once living to walk and work, to embrace others in friendship and love, to parent children of their own, to break bread and to give thanks. For the ancient Greeks, their view of the soul escaping from the body at the time of death meant that the body could be discarded as a husk, a mere shell. But not so among those who affirm the goodness of the body and the eventual resurrection of the body. In his fine book *The Undertaking,* funeral director Thomas Lynch takes aim at the "just a shell" treatment of the human body. He writes the following:

> There's this 'just a shell' theory of how we ought to relate to dead bodies. You hear a lot of it from young clergy, old family friends, well-intentioned in-laws—folks who are unsettled by the fresh grief

of others. You hear it when you bring a mother
and father in for the first sight of their dead daughter killed in a car wreck or left out to rot by some
mannish violence. It is proffered as comfort in the
teeth of what is a comfortless situation, consolation
to the inconsolable. Right between the inhale and
the exhale of the bone-wracking sob such hurts
produce, some frightened and well-meaning igno-
ramus is bound to give out with "It's OK, that's
not her, it's just a shell." I once saw an Episcopalian
deacon nearly decked by a swift slap of a mother
of a teenager, dead of leukemia, to whom he'd
tendered this counsel. "I'll tell you when *it's* 'just
a shell,'" the woman said. "For now and until I
tell you otherwise, she's my daughter."[19]

Jewish liturgical scholar Catherine Madsen por-
trays the Jewish tradition, out of which Christianity
grows, as one "whose bodiless God takes an insa-
tiable interest in the doings of human bodies."[20]
She goes on to describe the deep reverence shown
to dead bodies in ritual of *Tahara,* the preparation
of Jewish dead for burial, as it is observed in some
settings. A small group of people, known as *Chevra
Kadisha,* the "holy society," take on the responsibil-
ity of preparing the dead, she says. Men prepare
men, and women prepare women. The deceased

is addressed by his or her Hebrew name, and forgiveness is requested for any indignity that may inadvertently happen as they work. They wash the body twice, once with warm water and once with cold, and then the body is clothed in the garments of a Temple priest. Unembalmed, the body is placed in a wooden coffin made with pegs (so that nothing will impede the return of the body to the earth). "But the most disorienting feature of this profoundly disorienting ritual," writes Madsen, "occurs during the warm washing, when verses are sung from the Song of Songs":

His head is fine gold; his hair is curly and black as the raven.
His eyes are as doves by waterbrooks, washed in milk, set like jewels.
His cheeks are as beds of spices, yielding scent; his lips as lilies dropping myrrh.
His hands are rods of gold set with beryl; his belly a tablet of ivory inlaid with sapphires.
His legs are pillars of marble in sockets of gold.
He is like Lebanon, fine as the cedars.
His mouth is sweetness, and he is altogether lovely.
This is my beloved and this is my friend, O daughters of Jerusalem.[21]

Song of Songs 5:11–16

Christians have inherited from their Jewish forebears this profound reverence for the human body as a gift from God, a gift to be treated with gratitude both in life and in death.

What happens in the resurrection of the dead?— According to the gospel story, Jesus, who was buried with reverence in the traditional manner, did not remain in his tomb long. Early in the morning on the first day of the week, the third day after his death on Friday, the women who came to adorn his body with spices found that the tomb was empty and were astonished by the message of an angel in the cemetery, "Do not be afraid; I know that you are looking for Jesus who was crucified. He is not here, for he has been raised, as he said."

Right away, it is important to note two aspects of this claim of the resurrection of Jesus. First, it was not the idea of Jesus, or the spirit of Jesus, or the memory of Jesus, or the example of Jesus that was raised from the dead—it was Jesus himself, the embodied Jesus. Some argue that the New Testament describes some kind of "spiritualized" resurrection, but the Gospels are at pains to say otherwise. The risen Jesus eats food in the presence of the disciples (Luke 24:43); he shows the disciples his wounded body and invites Thomas to touch him (John 20:20, 27); the disciples put their hands on his feet (Matt. 28:9); and Jesus says to them, "Look at my hands and my feet; see that it is I myself. Touch me and see; for a ghost does not have flesh and bones as you see that I have" (Luke 24:38–39). Jesus's resurrection is not merely the resurrection of his spirit; it is a resurrection of his body.

But even though it was Jesus himself, the embodied Jesus, who was raised, we must also say—and this is the second important aspect of the resurrection to note—that the risen Jesus was not merely a resuscitated Jesus. The idea in popular piety that Jesus was walking around alive on Thursday, was crucified on Friday, and then was walking around again, good as new, on Sunday, is wrong and misses what the New Testament is trying to describe. The Gospel writers want to show that the risen Jesus was both continuous and discontinuous with the Jesus who spoke the beatitudes, preached in parables, healed the sick, and fed the multitudes. Yes, the risen Jesus was raised in body, but it was a changed body, a transfigured body, a glorified body.

How did the New Testament writers communicate that the risen Jesus was the same and yet different, that he was embodied but with a new and glorified body? The answer is not by writing a theological essay on transfiguration, but it is instead by telling the story first this way and then that way. Like riding a bicycle, the gospel writers kept the story moving by pushing down on the pedal on one side and then pushing down on the pedal on the opposite side. So, the risen Jesus was recognized by his followers (e.g., Matt. 28:9), and yet he was also not recognized by them (e.g., Luke 24:16; John 20:14). He had a body of flesh and bones and an appetite (e.g., Luke 24:39–43), and yet he passes through locked doors and appears and disappears abruptly (e.g., John 20:19; Luke 24:31). He invites his followers to touch him (e.g., Luke 24:39; John 20:27), and he also forbids them to hold onto him (John 20:17). In writing this way, the Gospel writers were not speaking out of both sides of their mouths. Rather they were trying to use ordinary words to describe the indescribable: how the resurrection of Jesus was the raising of the Jesus the disciples knew but was also the presence of something altogether new and unprecedented, the disruption of the temporal by the eternal.

This is why some theologians, for example Karl Barth, say that the resurrection of Jesus happened *in* history but that it was not *of* history. Barth writes the following:

> In the Resurrection the new world of the Holy Spirit touches the old world of the flesh, but touches it as a tangent touches a circle, that is, without touching it. And precisely because it does not touch it, it touches it as its frontier—as the new world. The Resurrection is, therefore, an occurrence in history, which took place outside the gates of Jerusalem in the year A.D. 30. . . . But inasmuch as the occurrence was conditioned by the Resurrection . . . the Resurrection is not an event in history at all.[22]

In his painting *The Resurrection of Christ*, the Italian Renaissance painter Tintoretto attempts to capture in paint the merging of the eternal and the temporal in this event.

As I have written elsewhere about this painting,[23]

In the Upper Hall of the Scuola Grande di San Rocco in Venice hangs Tintorello's striking painting

"The Resurrection of Christ." The scene is set at the rock tomb at dawn on Easter morning. Christ rises in a blaze of light as angels swirl around the mouth of the tomb. In the early morning darkness, the guards lie on the ground, either asleep or paralyzed with fear, and in the background, the two Marys can be seen making their way to the place of burial.

A remarkable feature of this painting is that, while all of the characters obviously are represented on the same canvas, the risen Christ seems to occupy a separate plane of reality than do the others. Charles Taylor, commenting on this painting in his magisterial book *A Secular Age,* says, "The figure of Christ emerging from the tomb is in a zone of sharp discontinuity from the rest of the picture where the guards are."[24] It is almost as if the canvas has a hole ripped in it just above the area depicting the tomb and that light streams through this hole from another realm, indeed from another time. The risen Christ is embedded in that light. "[S]ome break in the painting," says Taylor, "allows us to see the irruption of higher time."[25]

This discussion about eternity and temporality is not simply a parlor game for theologians, it is rather a response to a common misconception about resurrection. Many Christians believe that Easter is about the claim that God one day reached into history, plucked the dead Jesus from the tomb, and made him alive again. In a scientific age, such a view makes the resurrection of Jesus a kind of divine magic trick, a temporary interruption of the so-called "laws of nature," one of those laws being that dead people stay dead. This magic-trick view is one of the chief reasons that many honest Christians find the resurrection hard to swallow and have to get off the subway of credulity at the stop before Easter.

But the resurrection of Jesus is not an intrusion into the way things are, a momentary interruption of the laws of physics and biology. The resurrection of Jesus is a *disclosure* of the way things truly are. The resurrection of Jesus is not a one-time exception. It is a revelation in the experience of Easter of the ways things always are in the life of God and, therefore, in a creation held and sustained by God.

Because the resurrection of Jesus is a disclosure, and because it is an event, as Barth says, that is *in* history but not *of* history, people do not come to resurrection faith by reasoning or logical proof. When the early Christian preachers said of Jesus, "God raised him up," as Peter preached on the Day of Pentecost, it was not a statement like "water boils at 100 degrees centigrade under standard pressure," a scientific claim that can be tested in the lab. The announcement of the resurrection is a claim, something closer to "I love you" or "You know your mother would be proud of you now." These are not statements that can be proved by scientific methods, but they are claims upon us that, if believed to be true, are potentially life changing.

The disciples and others among the earliest followers of Jesus encountered the risen Christ. As we have said, he was definitely the same Jesus they had known, but he was also different. There was continuity and discontinuity, familiarity and newness. He was a human being, but he was also the risen and glorified Lord. They told the story of their encounters to others. They preached about their encounters in their sermons. Some people believed what they heard and others did not. The story of the resurrection of Jesus continues to be told to this day, and with the same results. Some believe and others do not. For those who do believe, the word "belief" becomes too small. One's relationship to the risen Christ is better described as "trust" and "faith." One wagers one's life on the truth of the resurrection and rests one's hope in its promise. And then something remarkable happens: the eyes of faith begin to perceive evidence of the life-giving power of God all around. Once one trusts that God brought life from death in Jesus, one begins to see God bringing life from death every day—in the healing of disease, the toppling of tyrants, the reconciliation of enemies, and more. We do not add up the evidence and then, on the basis of it come to faith in the resurrection. It works the other way. We come to faith, and then the evidence becomes visible. As the theologian Anselm said, "Faith seeking understanding."

When we look at creation through the lens of the resurrection, we see that God has created a world that operates by resurrection and prayer just as surely as it operates by gravity and thermodynamics, a world that is held and sustained by the loving and merciful God who forever brings life out of death.[26] To the skeptical voice who mutters under his breath on Easter, "Oh come on, get *real*," the resurrection announces, "No, look, *this* is what is real. This fullness, this promise, this life, *is* reality when one knows how to see."

This is why the faith has always claimed that the resurrection of Jesus is not just the experience of one human being but is also the promise of resurrection for us, too. "For as all die in Adam," wrote Paul, "so all will be made alive in Christ" (1 Cor. 15:22). Elsewhere Paul picks up the same theme: "For if we have been united with him in a death like his, we will certainly be united with him in a resurrection like his."

Just as Jesus's risen body was both like and unlike his earlier body, our bodies will be transformed as well. "We will be changed," said Paul, "For this perishable body, must put on imperishability." For many years, Christian theologians imagined that this putting on imperishability meant that God would gather up a person's remains, the decaying body in the grave, and transform the physical elements of the old body in the new and glorified body. There was, therefore, a long-standing resistance to cremation in the Christian tradition, lest the body be damaged beyond all hope of transformation. Even before the advent of modern science, though, theologians recognized some problems with this view. Augustine, who thought a great deal about how this process of bodily glorification would occur, was troubled, for example, about what this meant for aborted fetuses who never had a living body outside the womb, or for children who never achieved an adult body, or for the aged whose bodies were feeble. He finally decided that God would raise human beings not as their bodies were at the time of death but as their bodies were or would have been at their prime, about thirty years of age![27]

In a scientific time, the questions become even more vexing. We know that human bodies are not static but are in flux, ever-changing entities. Cells die and new cells are born. Which body gets raised? The one we have this week? Next week? Also, human beings leave cells and DNA on everything we touch. A person who eats a meal at a restaurant leaves part of the body behind on the cups and plates. Does God gather up this scattered bodily residue at the time of resurrection? And then there is the old and mildly disgusting dorm room quandary: suppose a cannibal eats a missionary, and suppose the missionary's body is digested and incorporated into the body of the cannibal. Then, later the cannibal later repents and comes to faith. Whose body gets raised?

More recently, theologians have reframed this question of bodily resurrection. The point is not that every scrap of a person's old body—bones, flesh, blood, and spittle—is somehow scraped together and repurposed as a glorified body. Rather, the resurrection of the body is the promise that what is essential to embodied human life is also true about the resurrected life. If someone wants to know who I am, then observe what I do with my body. With my body I go here but not there, I embrace this one in love and faithful commitment and not the other, I labor and I rest, I speak this way and not another way. Through my body, I have agency and memory, I form relationships with others, and I belong to others in community. I do not make sense or have substance apart from my embodied life. We do not know what our resurrected bodies will be like, but we do know they will enable us to be the purposeful and relational persons that our bodies now allow us to be. Understanding resurrection embodiment in this way, incidentally, has permitted many Christian to be more open to cremation, and the percentage rates of cremation have increased dramatically.

The resurrection of the body is a validation of the embodied life each of us has lived and a perfection of that life in glory. New Testament scholar Dale C. Allison Jr. describes it in the following way:

> That we will, if we continue to exist, be our true selves only in community is a sensible projection from life as we now know it, and it's a projection encouraged by the image of bodily resurrection. For our bodies are more than biological machines. They are also the vehicles by which we establish and maintain social relationships. Bodies make it possible for us to know others and for others to know us. So profession of the resurrection is a way of saying that the world to come will be, like this one, communal. . . . Even after death we are members of one another.[28]

So, if we want to know who a person truly is in this life, then watch what they do in and through their bodies—the actions they take, the relationships they form, and the words they speak. But even so, something about the true nature of a person remains hidden from view. A brighter light is needed to see who a person really is, and that light is the resurrection. We look at others not simply as they are, but as they will be in the radiance of the resurrection. There is an old spiritual with the following lyrics:

> O, nobody knows who I am, a-who I am, till the
> Judgement morning
> Heaven bells a-ringing, the saints all singing
> Heaven bells a-ringing in my soul
> If you don't believe
> That I've been redeemed
> Follow me down
> To Jordan's stream.

What this old spiritual affirms is the deep theological truth that we are fully known only in the light of the resurrection. In his resurrection, Jesus appears to our gaze as he truly is, but also the risen Jesus sees us as we truly are in the unblinking love of God. As theologian and former archbishop of Canterbury Rowan Williams says the following:

> You have an identity not because you have invented one, or because you have a little hardcore of selfhood that is unchanged, but because you have a witness of who you are. What you don't understand or see, the bits of yourself you can't pull together in a convincing story, are all held together

45

in a single gaze of love. You don't have to work out and finalize who you are, and have been; you don't have to settle the absolute truth of your history or story. In the eyes of the presence that never goes away, all that you have been and are is still present and real; it is held together in that unifying gaze . . . the divine observer, the divine witness.[29]

This is not to say, of course, that all we bring to the divine gaze is lovely. We are all sinners, and all of us have misused our bodies and caused wreckage to ourselves and others. This is why the scriptures tell us that to be gathered up into the power of the resurrection is not only to be affirmed but also to be changed, transformed, healed, redeemed and purified. This is behind the biblical image of the fire of judgment, for example in 1 Corinthians:

> For no one can lay any foundation other than the one that has been laid; that foundation is Jesus Christ. Now if anyone builds on the foundation with gold, silver, precious stones, wood, hay, straw— the work of each builder will become visible, for the Day will disclose it, because it will be revealed with fire, and the fire will test what sort of work each has done. If what has been built on the foundation survives, the builder will receive a reward. If the work is burned up, the builder will suffer

loss; the builder will be saved, but only as through fire. (1 Cor. 3:11–15)

Notice that the fire in this passage is not the angry wildfire of "hellfire and damnation" preaching but rather the fire that burns away stubble, the fire that purifies. It is not a damning fire but a saving fire, because the fire is the risen Christ, who burns to reveal the image of God in each of us beneath the disfigurement of where we have gone astray. Who we truly are, said Joseph Ratzinger, the Catholic theologian who eventually became Pope Benedict XVI,

> is buried under a great deal of wood, hay, and straw. Only with difficulty can it peer out from behind the latticework of an egoism we are powerless to pull down with our own hands. Encounter with the Lord . . . is the fire that burns away our dross and re-forms us to be vessels of eternal joy.[30]

What does it look like, then, this redeemed and embodied resurrected existence? We see through a glass darkly here. Our only evidence about this new life, the risen Jesus himself, required that our most faithful witnesses speak in two ways: the risen Christ was both like his old self and unlike his old self. He spoke and acted in ways so familiar we recognized him, and yet his presence was so new and unexpected, we didn't recognize him. But this we do know: his was an embodied presence, and so shall ours be.

When will the resurrection happen? Once again, the New Testament appears to be of two main minds, this time on the question of when the dead are raised. When Jesus says to the thief on the cross, "Truly I tell you, today you will be with me in Paradise," (Luke 23:43), the implication is that the resurrection occurs immediately at the time of death. Paul, however, gives a dramatically different picture:

> For the Lord himself, with a cry of command, with the archangel's call and with the sound of God's trumpet, will descend from heaven, and the dead in Christ will rise first. Then we who are alive, who are left, will be caught up in the clouds together with them to meet the Lord in the air; and so we will be with the Lord forever. (1 Thess. 4:16–17)

Here the resurrection happens at the end of all things, to everyone all at once.

Both views have virtues and drawbacks. The view in Paul of a communal resurrection has the advantage of seeing the resurrection of the dead as part and parcel of God's promise to renew all of creation. The Easter promise is not just about people being raised one by one but about God making all things new. On the other hand, the communal view leaves the present dead in a kind of strange limbo. Some have portrayed this as being "asleep in Jesus," but what can that possibly mean? Are the dead with Jesus? If so, then they are gathered up in the power of the resurrection. Are they not with Jesus? Then the dead are alone and abandoned, and death has not been defeated.

Actually, the dilemma is an artificial one created by the sheer fact that we are creatures of history and confined to the limits of linear time. For us, events always happen chronologically, one after the other—first, second, third, and so on. But God is not a creature of time. Time is a creation of God, and not the other way around. "To God," as theologian Thomas Aquinas argued, "things are never future but always present."[31] So, for us to say that our grandmother was raised from the dead at the hour of her departure and also to say that she will be raised together with all the dead at the end of all things seems incommensurate. But actually, in the timelessness of God's life, they are both true, and to say them together is to affirm that they are held together in the eternal present of God.

An example from contemporary physics can serve as a parable of this truth. Imagine a train moving slowly down a railroad track. The train has, among its cars, a boxcar with its side removed. Observers beside the track, then, can see inside the boxcar, and what they see is a woman standing exactly in the middle of the boxcar. In front of her is a table, and on the table is a projector, also positioned precisely at the mid-point of the boxcar. The projector has two lenses, one pointing forward and the other backward. Now, suppose that at the very moment the woman on the boxcar passes by a man standing beside the track, she flips on the projector and light streams forward and backward. Here's the question: which wall of the boxcar does the light strike first? The forward wall? The back wall? Both walls at the same time? The answer, as Einstein's theories have taught us, is relative. For the woman on the train, who is moving with the train and the projector, the light strikes both walls at the same time. But for the man standing beside the track, who is not moving, the light strikes the back wall first, because that wall is moving toward the streaming light while the front wall is moving away from it. In other words, both are true; the light strikes the back wall first and both walls simultaneously, depending upon where the observer is standing.

If time is not a fixed thing even in the world of physics, how much more can we imagine that time in the life of God is not bound to our notions of chronology and linearity. Was the thief who hung on the cross beside Jesus raised to new life on that very day or will that happen at the end of time? Yes.

What is life like for those who are resurrected? We can forget all the cartoon images of saints with halos and harps floating on clouds, and we can put aside all the jokes about St. Peter at the gates and resurrected golfers happily teeing off on the heavenly links. It is equally mistaken to take with wooden literalism even the beautiful images of the heavenly Jerusalem, with streets paved with gold, found in Revelation:

> The wall [of the heavenly city] is built of jasper, while the city is pure gold, clear as glass. The foundations of the wall of the city are adorned with every jewel; the first was jasper, the second sapphire, the third agate, the fourth emerald, the fifth

onyx, the sixth carnelian, the seventh chrysolite, the eighth beryl, the ninth topaz, the tenth chrysoprase, the eleventh jacinth, the twelfth amethyst. And the twelve gates are twelve pearls, each of the gates is a single pearl, and the street of the city is pure gold, transparent as glass. (Rev. 21:19–21)

Heaven is not a place like Des Moines or Buenos Aries. It is a symbol for the abundant life of God, into which the children of God are raised. We are not given any precise definitions of what that life is like, but we are given some guides to our imaginations.

We know, for example, that the risen Jesus still had the wounds of the crucifixion on his body, which guides us to imagine that the history and memory of this life, even its suffering, will not be forgotten but will be remembered and transformed. In Marilynne Robinson's novel *Gilead,* John Ames, an aging pastor, says that he has been thinking a great deal about this present life and existence:

> I know this [present life] is all mere apparition compared to what awaits us, but it is only lovelier for that. There is a human beauty in it. And I can't believe that, when we have all been changed and put on incorruptibility, we will forget our fantastic

condition of mortality and impermanence, the great bright dream of procreating and perishing that meant the whole world to us. In eternity this world will be Troy, I believe, and all that has passed here will be the epic of the universe, the ballad they sing in the streets. Because I don't imagine any reality putting this one in the shade entirely, and I think piety forbids me to try.[32]

What Ames imagines is that, in the life of resurrection, we will remember this life, but that it will no longer be a tale of meaningless suffering and the tragic unfolding of history. It will be a ballad, a song about the making of the saints.

If there is memory, then will we know our loved ones in that life to come? When my father died, a good number of people comforted me with the thought that he was now reunited with my mother, who had died eight years before. It was a nice thought in a time of grief, but it runs up against Jesus's own teaching, "For in the resurrection they neither marry nor are given in marriage, but are like angels in heaven." Once again, we are reminded that the resurrection life is a transformed life, not simply our old lives repeated for eternity. We are also reminded that, while some of us might be quite pleased to fellowship with our families in the world to come, those who have suffered abandonment or family violence might not see this as a blessing. What can we imagine then? Because there is memory in the resurrection, and because part of each person's embodiment consists of the relationships they have formed, we can only imagine that, yes, one will remember and recognize those people who have been a part of us and our lives. However, it will be a redeemed memory, and these will be transformed relationships. As Luther was reported to have said near the end of his own life, "We shall know our parents, wives, children, and everything else much more perfectly than Adam knew Eve."[33]

One other guide to our imagination about the life to come can be named: the resurrected life happens in community. The pictures in Revelation are not at all of individual saints on desert islands but of the gathering of a congregation, row upon row and rank upon rank (see Rev. 7). This community is not merely reflective of civic good will. It is rather because the very life of the Trinitarian God is communal, and to be raised is to be gathered into that life where the persons of the Trinity relate to each other in self-giving love. Sometimes heaven is pictured in static terms, like an eternal prayer meeting. But the images in scripture are of movement, energy, praise, and activity.

The character Jayber Crow in Wendell Berry's novel of the same name is the town barber and grave digger in the little town of Port William, Kentucky. He is also a deeply spiritual man, one who perceives the intersection of ordinary life and the eternal. One day, he goes up to the church to work in the graveyard, but he becomes sleepy. So he goes into the church and lies down on floor behind the back pew. In his drowsy state, he has a lovely and dream-like vision of what the heavenly beloved community might be like. He says the following:

> Waking or sleeping (I couldn't tell which), I saw all the people there who had ever been there. I saw them as I had seen them from the back pew, where I sat with Uncle Othy . . . while Aunt Cordie sang in the choir and I saw them as I had seen them (from the back pew) on the Sunday before. I saw them in all the times past and to come, all somehow there in their own time and in all time and in no time: the cheerfully working and singing women, the men quiet, reluctant or

shy, the weary, the troubled in spirit, the sick, the lame, the desperate, the dying, the little children tucked into the pews beside their elders, the young married couple full of visions, the old men with their dreams, the parents proud of their children, grandparents with tears in their eyes, the pairs of young lovers attentive only to each other on the edge of the world, the grieving widows and widowers, the mothers and fathers of children newly dead, the proud, the humble, the attentive, the distracted,—I saw them all. I saw the creases crisscrossed on the backs of the men's necks, their work-thickened hands, the Sunday dresses faded with washing.

They were all just there. They said nothing and I said nothing. I loved them all with a love that was mine merely because it included me.[34]

And then later, Jayber remembers this vision in the church, and what he says about it can serve as a fitting ending to our reflections: "And yet I saw them all as somehow perfected, beyond time, by one another's love, compassion, and forgiveness. As it is said we may be perfected by grace."[35]

Notes

1 Atul Gawande, *Being Mortal: Medicine and What Matters at the End* (New York: Metropolitan Books, 2014).

2 As quoted in Sherwin Nuland, *How We Die: Reflections of Life's Final Chapter* (New York: Vintage, 1995), 44.

3 Gawande, *Being Mortal,* 31.

4 Sara Davidson, "A Longer, Better Life," *New York Times Magazine* (May 6, 2007): 55.

5 Wallace Stegner, *The Spectator Bird,* rev. ed. (New York: Penguin Classic, 2010), 115.

6 Nuland, *How We Die,* 40–41.

7 Ibid., 84.

8 Benedict XVI, "Homily," Saint Peter's Basilica, Holy Saturday, April 3, 2010, accessed at http://w2.vatican.va/content/benedict-xvi/en/homilies/2010/documents/hf_ben-xvi_hom_20100403_veglia-pasquale.html.

9 Michel de Montaigne, *The Complete Essays of Montaigne* (Stanford, CA: Stanford University Press, 1958), 67.

10 Quoted in Anatole Broyard, *Intoxicated by My Illness, and Other Writings on Life and Death* (New York: Fawcett, 1993), 78.

11 Ibid., 45.

12 Nuland, *How We Die,* xvi–xvii.

13 Ibid., 242.

14 Ernest Becker, *The Denial of Death* (New York: The Free Press, 1973), 285.

15 Oliver Sacks, "The Joy of Old Age. (No Kidding.)," *New York Times,* July 6, 2013, SR12.

16 Oliver Sacks, "Sabbath," *New York Times*, August 16, 2015, SR1.

17 Lisa Miller, *Visions of Heaven; A Journey through the Afterlife* (New York: Time, 2014), 82.

18 Miller, *Visions of Heaven,* 34.

19 Thomas Lynch, *The Undertaking: Life Studies from the Dismal Trade* (New York: W. W. Norton, 1997), 20–21.

20 Catherine Madsen, "Love Songs to the Dead: The Liturgical Voice as Mentor and Reminder," *Cross Currents* 48/4 (Winter 1998–1999), 459.

21 Ibid.

22 Karl Barth, *The Epistle to the Romans* (Oxford: Oxford University Press, 1968), 30.

23 Thomas G. Long, "Preaching the Gospel of Resurrection," *Preaching Gospel: Essays in Honor of Richard Lischer* (Eugene, OR: Cascade Books, 2016), 73.

24 Charles Taylor, quoted in ibid., 97.

25 Ibid., 145.

26 See Janet Martin Soskice, "God of Power and Might," *Theology Today* 54/1 (1997), 19–28.

27 Augustine, *City of God,* Book XXII: 13–16.

28 Dale C. Allison Jr. *Night Comes: Death, Imagination, and the Last Things* (Grand Rapids, MI: Eerdmans, 2016), 41–42.

29 Rowan Williams, *Being Disciples: Essentials of the Christian Life* (Grand Rapids, MI: Eerdmans, 2016), 29.

30 Joseph Ratzinger, *Eschatology: Death and Eternal Life* (Washington: Catholic University of America Press, 1988), 231.

31 Thomas Aquinas, *Deo Verifate;* cited by David B. Burrell, *Knowing the Unknowable God: Ibn-Sinu, Muimonides, Aquinas* (Notre Dame: University of Notre Dame Press,1986), 100.

32 Marilynne Robinson, *Gilead* (New York: Picador, 2006), 66.

33 Luther as quoted in Johannes Sledianus, *The General History of the Reformation of the Church, from the Errors and Corruptions of the Church of Rome* (London: Edw. Jones, 1689), 362. See also Allison, *Night Comes,* 134–138.

34 Walker Percy, *Jayber Crow* (Washington: Counterpoint, 2000), 164–165.

35 Ibid., 205.